About Demos

Who we are

Demos is the think tank for everyday democracy. We believe everyone should be able to make personal choices in their daily lives that contribute to the common good. Our aim is to put this democratic idea into practice by working with organisations in ways that make them more effective and legitimate.

What we work on

We focus on six areas: public services; science and technology; cities and public space; people and communities; arts and culture; and global security.

Who we work with

Our partners include policy-makers, companies, public service providers and social entrepreneurs. Demos is not linked to any party but we work with politicians across political divides. Our international network – which extends across Eastern Europe, Scandinavia, Australia, Brazil, India and China – provides a global perspective and enables us to work across borders.

How we work

Demos knows the importance of learning from experience. We test and improve our ideas in practice by working with people who can make change happen. Our collaborative approach means that our partners share in the creation and ownership of new ideas.

What we offer

We analyse social and political change, which we connect to innovation and learning in organisations. We help our partners show thought leadership and respond to emerging policy challenges.

How we communicate

As an independent voice, we can create debates that lead to real change. We use the media, public events, workshops and publications to communicate our ideas. All our books can be downloaded free from the Demos website.

www.demos.co.uk

First published in 2006
© Demos
Some rights reserved – see copyright licence for details

ISBN 1 84180 157 7
Copy edited by Julie Pickard
Typeset by utimestwo, Collingtree, Northants
Printed by Upstream, London

For further information and
subscription details please contact:

Demos
Magdalen House
136 Tooley Street
London SE1 2TU

telephone: 0845 458 5949
email: hello@demos.co.uk
web: www.demos.co.uk

Cultural Value and the Crisis of Legitimacy

Why culture needs a democratic mandate

John Holden

Supported by

CALOUSTE
GULBENKIAN
FOUNDATION

DEM◉S

DEM⊙S

Contents

Acknowledgements

This publication would not have been possible without the support of the United Kingdom branch of the Calouste Gulbenkian Foundation, and I am most grateful to everyone at the Gulbenkian for their support.

I am also greatly indebted to the many people, too numerous to mention individually, with whom I have discussed the ideas contained in this pamphlet.

My colleagues at Demos have been a constant source of stimulation. Tom Bentley, Paul Skidmore, Charlie Tims and Shelagh Wright deserve special mention, but Sam Jones has been of immense help, both intellectually and in assisting with the production. Thanks for the production and dissemination of this pamphlet to Eddie Gibb, Sam Hinton-Smith, Abi Hewitt, Julia Huber and the Demos interns. In addition I have received help and assistance from Justine Simons of the Mayor's Office and Professor Sara Selwood of City University; but my largest debt is owed to my frequent collaborator and friend Robert Hewison for his editing skills, insights and unfailing encouragement.

John Holden
March 2006

8   Demos

1. Summary

The 'cultural system' faces a crisis of legitimacy. At local government level culture is suffering extreme funding cuts,[1] the recent Arts Council England (ACE) *Peer Review* uncovers a rift between ACE and its Whitehall department,[2] and individual organisations continue to stagger from one damning headline to the next.[3] These are the current symptoms of a deeper problem that has dogged culture for the last 30 years.

Politics has struggled to understand culture and failed to engage with it effectively. Cultural professionals have focused on satisfying the policy demands of their funders in an attempt to gain the same unquestioning support for culture that exists for health or education; but the truth is that politicians will never be able to give that support until there exists a more broadly based and better articulated democratic consensus.

The diagnosis is worrying, but the prognosis is optimistic. 'Cultural value' has provided politicians with an understanding of why culture is important, and is helping institutions to explain themselves, and to talk to each other.

The language and conceptual framework provided by 'cultural value' tell us that publicly funded culture generates three types of value: intrinsic value, instrumental value and institutional value. It explains that these values play out – are created and 'consumed' –

within a triangular relationship between cultural professionals, politicians, policy-makers and the public.

But the analysis illuminates a problem: politicians and policy-makers appear to care most about instrumental economic and social outcomes, but the public and most professionals have a completely different set of concerns.

As a result the relationships between the public, politicians and professionals have become dysfunctional. The 'cultural system' has become a closed and ill-tempered conversation between professionals and politicians, while the news pages of the media play a destructive role between politics and the public.

The problems are clearly systemic but the solutions must start with cultural professionals. Their opportunity is that the value of culture to the public is unlimited and infinitely expandable. The challenge, which is already being taken up in some places, is to create a different alignment between culture, politics and the public. In practice this will require courage, confidence and radicalism on the part of professionals in finding new ways to build greater legitimacy directly with citizens. The evidence so far suggests that such an approach would be successful and would serve the aims of all concerned – politicians, the professionals themselves, and above all the public.

2. Introduction

What is culture?

No one would suggest that defining culture is easy. Raymond Williams in *Keywords* says that 'culture is one of the two or three most complicated words in the English Language',[4] and government certainly struggles. The Department for Culture, Media and Sport's (DCMS's) website admits 'There is no official government definition of "culture".[5] Efforts have begun at various levels – from UNESCO, to the European Union, to DCMS itself – to tackle this issue of language and definition, and progress is being made, but as the DCMS's *Evidence Toolkit* insists, when it comes to culture, 'There are no shared definitions, systems and methodologies.'[6] Yet in practice definitions *are* used by policy-makers at national, regional and local levels. The definitions flow from administrative convenience, and do not match people's everyday understanding and experience of culture. Who on the high street would think that sport or tourism came under the heading 'culture', or that antique dealing was a 'creative industry'? This in itself illustrates the gap that exists between the public and politics when it comes to culture.

In this paper I will use a narrow characterisation of culture to mean the arts, museums, libraries and heritage that receive public funding, although many of my arguments apply more broadly into the commercial arts and into other parts of the publicly funded sector.

The legitimacy of funding culture

In June 2003 Demos, along with AEA Consulting, the National Gallery and the National Theatre, held a conference called 'Valuing Culture'.[7] It was convened because many people had become frustrated by the fact that culture seemed to be valued by politicians only in terms of what it could achieve for other economic and social agendas. Somehow, over a period of decades, politics had mislaid the essence of culture, and policy had lost sight of the real meaning of culture in people's lives and in the formation of their identities. Soon afterwards the Secretary of State for Culture, Media and Sport, Tessa Jowell, who had spoken at the conference, published a personal essay, *Government and the Value of Culture*, in which she issued this challenge: 'How, in going beyond targets, can we best find a language to capture the value of culture?'[8] My own response was to write *Capturing Cultural Value*,[9] which sought to find just such a language by seeing what other people, such as environmentalists, anthropologists and accountants, were doing when faced with the same problem: how to find ways in which to express the value of things that are difficult or impossible to measure. 'Cultural value' helped to frame a new way of understanding, and therefore of evaluating and investing in culture, but it goes only part of the way to illuminating how the 'cultural system' can be improved. Shared understandings and a richer language are important, but there is another, even more fundamental, issue – that of legitimacy.

The fact is that government funding of culture, whether at national or local level, is not accepted in politics as a public good in the same way that health or education, for example, are. One simple fact makes it clear that politics has a problem with culture: over the past three decades, central government funding across the OECD countries has been erratic,[10] and the flow of funds into the sector has often been turned on and off not for financial reasons, but on ideological grounds. There is a nervousness about art and culture in our political discourse that results from a democratic deficit. Public approval of culture is hidden; politicians are scared off culture by the media; and cultural professionals have spent too much time in a closed conversation with their funders, feeding them with statistics and 'good stories'. The answer to the question 'why fund culture?' should be 'because the public wants it'. Until politicians understand what the public values about culture, and until cultural professionals create and articulate that demand, culture will always remain vulnerable to indifference or attack.

This essay attempts to generate a clearer exposition of cultural value and to articulate why culture matters in politics and public life. It exposes differences of interest in culture between politicians, cultural professionals and the public, but concludes that these differences are capable of being understood and reconciled to the benefit of all concerned. Clarifying these issues will help us to find ways in which the 'cultural system' can work better to generate value for the public. Many lovers of culture want to see unquestioning and consistent government support, both rhetorical and financial. They need to recognise that politicians fund what the public demands. If a sustainable base for culture is to be secured then cultural professionals need to think of 'advocacy' not just in terms of generating 'evidence' for their funders, but as establishing broad support with the public.

The analysis, and the structural context in which it sits in the UK (and in many other countries that are grappling with similar questions), suggests several priorities and prescriptions for change. These are explored throughout the following text, and in particular in the conclusion.

3. Cultural value

Publicly funded culture generates three types of value – intrinsic, instrumental and institutional. A more detailed discussion of these values and the difficulties of expressing them can be found in *Capturing Cultural Value*,[11] but they are summarised in the 'value triangle' shown in figure 1.

Intrinsic values

Intrinsic values are the set of values that relate to the subjective experience of culture intellectually, emotionally and spiritually. It is these values that people refer to when they say things such as 'I hate this; it makes me feel angry', or 'If this was taken away from me I would lose part of my soul', or 'This tells me who I am'. These kinds of values can be captured in personal testimony, qualitative assessments, anecdotes, case studies and critical reviews.

Because intrinsic values are experienced at the level of the individual they are difficult to articulate in terms of mass 'outcomes'. Consequently they present problems: how are they to be measured? How do we develop a consistent language to express intrinsic value? How do personal experiences translate into social phenomena and political priorities? Are there standards of quality that can be shared? What is the role of expert opinion?

In *Capturing Cultural Value* I attempted to debunk the old 'art for art's sake' idea that culture could have some value 'in and of itself'.

Figure 1 Value triangle

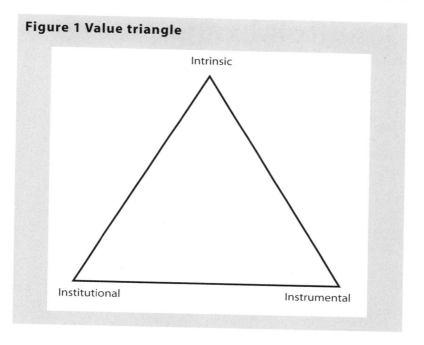

Intrinsic

Institutional   Instrumental

Instead, I maintained that value is located in the encounter or interaction between individuals (who will have all sorts of pre-existing attitudes, beliefs and levels of knowledge) on the one hand, and an object or experience on the other. Intrinsic values are better thought of then as the *capacity and potential* of culture to affect us, rather than as measurable and fixed stocks of worth.

But I did voice the opinion that it was vital to re-establish a convincing and serious language to talk about the way in which culture moves us. Shortly afterwards a report from the US RAND Corporation reached a similar conclusion, saying 'there is general awareness that these (instrumental) arguments ignore the intrinsic benefits the arts provide to individuals and the public. So far, however, little analysis has been conducted that would help inform public discourse about these issues.'[12] The *Los Angeles Times* summed up the RAND report in the following terms: 'After wading through stacks of economic and educational studies used to drum up arts funding, RAND Corp. researchers say the numbers don't make a persuasive case and that arts advocates should emphasize the intrinsic benefits that make people cherish the arts.'[13] As a first step towards answering that challenge, *Capturing Cultural Value* suggested that Professor David Throsby's categorisations of historical, social, symbolic, aesthetic and spiritual value would be a good starting point, because they break down a nebulous concept into more manageable terms expressed in everyday language.[14]

Instrumental values

Instrumental values relate to the ancillary effects of culture, where culture is used to achieve a social or economic purpose. They are often, but not always, expressed in figures. This kind of value tends to be captured in 'output', 'outcome' and 'impact' studies that document the economic and social significance of investing in the arts. They might, for example, be reflected in the amount of local employment created by a newly constructed cinema, the difference in truancy rates of pupils participating in an educational project, or the recovery times of patients who sing together. The problems of 'capturing' these outcomes are well documented in *Capturing Cultural Value* as well as in texts by Selwood, Ellis, Oakley, RAND, DCMS and Carey.[15] Briefly stated, the problems are as follows:

- o   Establishing a causal link between culture and a beneficial economic or social outcome is difficult because of temporal remoteness, complexity of the interaction, the context in which it takes place, and the multiplicity of other factors impacting on the result.
- o   There is little in the way of longitudinal evidence to support correlation between culture and its effects because cultural practice, the context in which it takes place and policy goals are constantly shifting.
- o   'Evidence' is often confused with advocacy.

○ It is virtually impossible to prove that, even if a cultural intervention works, it is the most direct and cost-effective way of achieving a particular social or economic aim.

Fundamentally these problems exist because, when it comes to instrumental benefits, culture creates potential rather than having a predictable effect.

Nonetheless, in spite of the difficulties with the evidence, much of the rationale for the public funding of culture rests on an appeal to its effectiveness in achieving instrumental aims. A clear example can be found in the agreement between Arts Council England and the Local Government Association, which states that their joint approach to the arts will focus on:

○ the creative economy
○ healthy communities
○ vital neighbourhoods
○ engaging young people.[16]

Capturing Cultural Value argues that culture does have significant instrumental value, but that instrumental value on its own does not give an adequate account of the value of culture, and that, moreover, better methodologies need to be found to demonstrate instrumental value in a convincing way.

Institutional value

Institutional value relates to the processes and techniques that organisations adopt in how they work to create value for the public. Institutional value is created (or destroyed) by how these organisations engage with their public; it flows from their working practices and attitudes, and is rooted in the ethos of public service. Through its concern for the public an institution can achieve such public goods as creating trust and mutual respect among citizens, enhancing the public realm, and providing a context for sociability and the enjoyment of shared experiences. Institutional value is akin to the idea of 'public value' as discussed in the work of Mark Moore.[17]

Institutional value sees the role of cultural organisations not simply as mediators between politicians and the public, but as active agents in the creation or destruction of what the public values. The responsible institutions themselves should be considered not just as repositories of objects, or sites of experience, or instruments for generating cultural meaning, but as creators of value in their own right. It is not the existence of a theatre or a museum that creates these values; they are created in the way that the organisation relates to the public to which, as a publicly funded organisation, it is answerable. Trust in the public realm, transparency and fairness, are all values that can be generated by the institution in its dealings with the public. This concern for increasing broad public goods, this care and concern for the public, is expressed in ways both large and, seemingly, small: a commitment to showing the whole of a collection in a fine building at one end of the scale, to serving hot drinks at the other. But it is through recognising these values, and, crucially, *deciding for itself* how to generate them, that the moral purpose of an organisation becomes apparent, and where organisational rhetoric meets reality.

Institutional value is evidenced in feedback from the public, partners and people working closely with the organisation. Although the idea of public value has come to the attention of policy-makers, ways of measuring and talking about *how* institutions add value have not yet been fully articulated or brought into everyday practice, except in a small number of institutions, most notably the BBC, where it has had profound effects.[18] Demos has been working with a number of organisations, such as the Heritage Lottery Fund and The Sage Gateshead, to understand and to bring out this set of values, exploring how theory and practice can develop in tandem with the benefit of organisations and the public.[19] In addition, a report by Morton Smyth Ltd, *Not for the Likes of You*, gives examples of institutional values developed in the context of audience development.[20]

Postwar cultural policy

In the immediate postwar era, publicly funded culture in Britain was largely elite and metropolitan. It was concerned with intrinsic values and had a strict hierarchy of worth. In 1959 the independent Bridges Report, *Help for the Arts*, recognised that culture needed to be less hierarchically organised and more regionally available.[21] In 1965, the Wilson government's white paper *Policy for the Arts* (the first of its kind in Britain) made this approach official.[22] There was substantial investment in the cultural infrastructure and the idea of art that promoted social goods – community arts, arts in education – arrived. With the advent of Thatcherism, culture came under attack both ideologically and financially, and was reduced to backward-looking nostalgia in the service of strictly instrumental economic ends. When New Labour came to power, a set of socially instrumental outcomes was added: in addition to regeneration and 'the creative economy', culture was expected to help reduce crime, promote lifelong learning and improve the nation's health.

But in the last two years there has been increasing recognition that instrumental values do not tell the whole story about culture, and that all three sorts of value need to be brought into account.[23] Intrinsic, instrumental and institutional values thus represent a kind of historical layering or interweaving. As discussed further in chapter 5, they also represent different aspects and concerns about culture, intrinsic value being metaphysical, instrumental political and institutional administrative.

The triangle in figure 1 then shows the three ways in which culture generates value; but each 'I' is problematic: the historic approach to the metrics of instrumental value are flawed; those of intrinsic value lack an adequate and consistent language of expression; and those of institutional value are almost completely undeveloped.

4. Cultural context

A second triangle (figure 2) sets out the relationship of the three parties involved in the cultural concordat:

○ the public
○ politicians and policy-makers
○ professionals.

When pared to its essentials the settlement about funded culture between the public, politicians and policy-makers at national and local level, and cultural professionals operates like this:

○ The public vote for politicians.
○ The politicians decide the legal and policy framework within which culture operates, and, crucially, decide the financial resources that they are prepared to commit.
○ The professionals do their work, and offer it to the public for consumption.
○ Funders occupy a space between professionals and politicians, with Arts Council England, for example, expected both to 'lead the arts sector and speak on its behalf', and to distribute government money in order to achieve government aims by 'show(ing) progress against PSA targets and the impact of government spending on the arts'.[24]

Figure 2 Relationship triangle

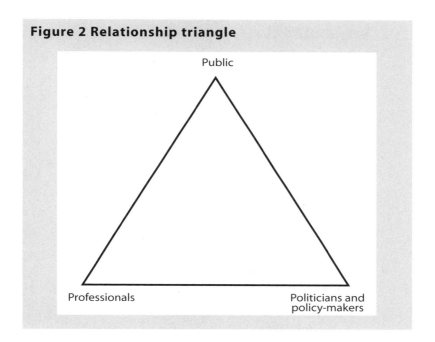

This model provided an adequate explanation of reality when people voted for Harold Macmillan, who gave money to the National Gallery; Kenneth Clark, or some other figure of cultural authority, then told the nation which pictures were beautiful, and the public either went to see them or stayed at home.

But that model no longer works. In order to explain why, we need to look at the changing nature of the public, politicians and policy-makers, and professionals, and at the changed relationships between them.

The public

The term 'the public' is useful in that it embraces all of us: we are all citizens and we all have an interest in public life and its expression through culture. But 'the public' is obviously not a unified field.

Everyone is now in a minority group, so we need to understand that the public has multiple identities and many voices, not just one.

The nature of 'the public' is changing rapidly and in ways that are profoundly significant for politicians and professionals:

O Economic and demographic trends are altering cultural consumption. Broadly speaking people have more money and less time, and more choices about how they spend both; they are increasingly looking for 'perfect moments' – low risk but high quality and exciting experiences.[25]

O The public contains and is exposed to a greater diversity of culture and cultural influences. Culture has thus become of increased importance in the formation of individual identities.

O Education and the 'cultural socialisation' of young people at school (ie their increasing familiarity with publicly funded culture through such things as museum visits and theatre workshops) will mean greater interest and participation in all forms of culture.[26]

O The public, as increasingly sophisticated consumers, are likely to be more demanding, and less forgiving of dowdy cultural infrastructure, poor service and over-inflated claims.

O The distinction between amateur and professional is disappearing as 'amateurs' attain 'professional' standards through access to better technology and means of communication,[27] and as professionals work more and more with 'amateurs'.[28]

But more significant than any of the above is the possibility that we are entering a time when the role of culture in society is undergoing a fundamental shift. Throughout the twentieth century we – the public – were defined by two things: our nationality and our work. In these circumstances culture was both a reassurance and a decoration. It was a reassurance because we lived in relatively homogenous societies with clear identities; the cultural markers were obvious and well understood. It was a decoration because it was offered as compensation for work, a leisure pursuit, something affordable after the serious business of the day was done.

In the twenty-first century all that has changed. Our nation states are far from homogenous; every individual citizen is now part of a minority; and we no longer define ourselves by our work – most of us will have different jobs, take career breaks, get re-educated, adjust our roles when children come along, and so on. In these circumstances we, the public, *need* culture more and more to make sense of our lives, and to construct our individual and collective identities. In addition, people have fluid identities, perhaps going to a rock concert at Knebworth one week and visiting the great house the next. In a globalised world with access to multiple, diverse and interwoven cultures, answers to the questions 'Who am I?'[29] and 'Who are we?' are found in people's cultural consumption (and increasingly in their cultural production). In turn that raises the stakes: the risk of participating in culture is not only financial; nowadays people also jeopardise their sense of self-esteem and self-definition.

Culture has become more important in questions of identity – but, perhaps paradoxically, its relationship to work has also become more important, as the cultural content of the knowledge and service economy grows ever greater.

What does the public value?

The public primarily values three things about culture.

The first is all those wonderful, beautiful, uplifting, challenging, stimulating, thought-provoking, terrifying, disturbing, spiritual, witty, transcendental experiences that shape and reflect their sense of self and their place in the world. They find these experiences in libraries as well as in theatres, in museums as well as in concert halls. The transcendental qualities of culture are not restricted to the publicly funded sector – they happen at rock concerts and West End musicals as well.

The second thing the public values is being treated well, and honestly, by the cultural organisations that they choose to engage with. They like decent catering at fair prices, and hate over-inflated claims about performances. They like good buildings and state-of-the-art technology. They want information and comfortable seats, and more and more they want participation of some kind.

The third thing of value to the public is the rootedness that culture provides. This can play out in two ways – in a sense of place and geographical location, where cultural infrastructure can anchor local identities, and in a sense of belonging to a community, either a geographical community, or a cultural community of interest.

On the whole, when it comes to culture the public do not directly care much (although indirectly they may care very much) about the things that politicians worry about: economic regeneration, social inclusion, healthy communities and the rest. They certainly do not think about culture in those terms, and do not use the language so often adopted by politicians and by professionals. As the RAND report puts it:

> *What draws people to the arts is not the hope that the experience will make them smarter or more self-disciplined. Instead it is the expectation that encountering a work of art can be a rewarding experience, one that offers them pleasure and emotional stimulation and meaning.*[30]

In terms of the 'value triangle' shown in figure 1 then, the public cares most about intrinsic value – at its simplest a good night out, at its best a spiritually moving experience – and to a degree about institutional value, because these two things construct and reflect their sense of who they are. But they do not care much about instrumental value.

Professionals

This category comprises all those people working in the cultural sphere; that is, within cultural organisations or involved individually in cultural endeavour. As with the public, this is far from being a unified field since professionals vary in their organisational contexts, backgrounds and motivations. The issue of motivation is crucial both in understanding where professionals think that they add value, and in interpreting their actions.

There are two points to note about the professionals. The first is that, in spite of the fact that some individuals may be very powerful, as a class their role has been undermined by a combination of factors: the decline of deference in society, the introduction of cultural relativism in postmodern thought, and the general attack on independent professionalism undertaken by governments around the world in the last 25 years.

The second point to acknowledge is the narrowing of the traditional divide between public and private sector models, structures and ethos in the lives of professionals:

o   In the publicly funded sector, young grant recipients often wonder why they have to set themselves up as a charity, and why they are not allowed to make money.

o   Entrepreneurs in the private sector 'subsidise' culture: a club owner in Newcastle puts on a commercial disco one night, and a non-commercial poetry reading the next.[31]

o   Conversely, organisations that sit in the public sphere, such as the Watershed in Bristol and the Public in West Bromwich (which will open in 2006), provide commercial spaces and collaborate with commercial enterprises.

o   Individual artists have always engaged with both public and private sectors (actors working in rep and TV for example, or sculptors selling their work to public galleries and to property developers), but now cultural organisations also make their living by selling commercial product, such as corporate training, as well as producing so-called 'subsidised' output.

o   It can be easily envisaged that a private sector cultural organisation will at some point take out an anti-competition action against a subsidised provider.

What do professionals value?

With all their diversity we should expect professionals to care about all three aspects of the value triangle, but not all professionals care about all three equally.

All are (or should be, for why otherwise would they be in the cultural sector?) motivated by intrinsic values, and by the quality of their work. Others, such as artists or organisations working in health or prisons or with particular social groups, are working towards worthwhile instrumental ends.[32] There is surely nothing wrong in using culture explicitly to reduce re-offending rates or to improve patient recovery times, as long as that is what the professionals have freely chosen to do, rather than been told to do, or obliged to pretend to do. But it is difficult to achieve instrumental ends in the absence of intrinsic value and, in order to achieve their instrumental aims, *all* professionals will seek to achieve the highest intrinsic quality in their work.

Similarly other professionals – particularly cultural leaders and facilities managers – will be most concerned with creating institutional value, but will recognise that if intrinsic value is absent, there will be no opportunity to create institutional value. Funders, too, should be concerned to generate their own institutional value in their relationships both with their political sponsors and their clients.

At heart then, professionals will be motivated by the intrinsic value and quality of a collection, a performance, an object or whatever art form they are involved with. In terms of the value triangle (figure 1), their organisational role will determine which aspects of value are important to them, but intrinsic value will be a *sine qua non*. As James Cuno, former director of the Courtauld Institute has put it, speaking of the Art Institute of Chicago:

> *The Art Institute represents one of those few institutions that has kept the course with regard to the unique contributions museums can make to the life of a city. It has done it in spite of other arguments: that it's socially therapeutic in some concrete ways or that it's an economic engine in some clear ways or that*

it's a site for privileged access, scholarly or whatever that might be. (The museum) is not any one of those things. . . . It engages all of them. But they are the result of the mission rather than being the mission itself.[33]

In the performing arts as well, the director of the National Theatre, Nicholas Hytner, has argued that intrinsic values should come first:

The orchestras were attacked not for the quality of their playing but for the unacceptably low proportion of young people in their audiences. There's evidently a thing called the young audience and everybody accepts that it's a good thing. And there's also a white, middle class, middle-aged audience and it's a very, very bad thing indeed. Until recently, the National Theatre's audience was getting worse reviews than some of its shows. Then somebody noticed some kids in the house with studs through their noses, and the reviews looked up. . . . We have to call a halt to this. There's nothing inherently good about any particular audience. We mustn't judge the success of an artistic enterprise by its ability to pull in an Officially Approved Crowd. . . . We want a diverse audience because we want a diverse repertoire. We want an audience that will support adventure, innovation, and that's always up for a challenge.[34]

Professionals need the satisfaction and authenticity that their pursuit of intrinsic values provides, but they also need other things: adequate pay, and respect from their peers, paymasters and public, among them. In that sense, they value a wider set of objectives, which they can achieve only by creating a different alignment between themselves, politicians and the public.

Politicians and policy-makers

Judging by references to the word in the discourse of politics, culture enjoys a lowly status across the political parties. In the last election the Labour manifesto devoted two short sections, each less than 200 words, to the arts and culture, in a section devoted to 'Quality of Life'. The Liberal Democrat manifesto mentions the word culture four times, and the topic 'Art, Heritage and Sport' is covered in about 100 words. The Conservative Party manifesto devoted 43 words to the arts, heritage and sport. A public opinion poll undertaken by MORI in May 2005 asked a number of questions of the public on the major issues confronting the electorate but culture did not feature.[35]

In terms of expenditure, too, culture lies at the political margins, accounting for 0.03 per cent of the European Union budget.[36] In the UK, the Arts Council England budget for 2005/06 amounts to £412 million.[37] By comparison, in 2003/04, cost *overruns* at the Ministry of Defence were more than seven times as much, at £3 billion.[38] Total UK departmental expenditure in 2004/05 amounted to £266 billion, of which the DCMS accounted for £1.4 billion, or 0.52 per cent. In terms of expenditure on services, recreation, culture and religion represented £6.9 billion of a total £485 billion for 2004/05.[39]

At local government level, the financing of culture lies at the margins; this is not surprising since culture is unfortunately not a statutory spending requirement (except for libraries), and funding is therefore easier to cut. According to a recent survey quoted in *Arts Professional*, 79 per cent of local government arts officers were expecting their budgets to be at standstill or to be cut. Eighteen English local authorities – one in 20 – have dispensed with their arts services completely since 2002.[40]

Politics finds culture difficult in other ways as well. Politics is concerned with mass social outcomes: it is about simplification and decision-making on a large scale. Art by contrast is about the individual, about complexity and subtlety. The former director of the National Theatre, Sir Richard Eyre, has pointed out that there is a fundamental incompatibility between politics and the arts. He quotes the American writer Philip Roth as saying:

> *Politics is the great generaliser and literature the great particulariser, and not only are they in an inverse relationship to each other they are in an antagonistic relationship. How can you*

be an artist and renounce the nuance? How can you be a politician and allow the nuance?[41]

Politics has attempted to side-step this difficulty by embracing culture as a transformative power for social good while simultaneously downplaying or ignoring its capacity to be disruptive and oppositional – a capacity that is surely part of culture's wider public value.

As we have seen, politics finds culture difficult to define, but we also have to recognise that the language used where culture and social policy meet is maddeningly obscure, riddled with jargon, not understood by some of the people who use it, and not understood by the public at all. Terms such as social inclusion, diversity, quality of life, health, well-being and community safety sometimes have technical meanings, sometimes not, but in any event the meanings are not widely shared. There is a huge disconnect between the public's idea of culture and what it is for, and the way that politics and policy talks about it.

In sum, politics and policy find culture to be:

○ a philosophical conundrum
○ linguistically difficult
○ incapable of definition
○ impossible to measure.

What do politicians and policy-makers value?

There is plenty of evidence from which to conclude that politicians primarily value culture for what it can achieve in terms of other, economic and social, agendas.[42] Although there *has* been a recent shift towards recognising that instrumental values do not tell the whole story – most notably in Tessa Jowell's personal essay *Government and the Value of Culture* – they continue to dominate the political discourse. For example, the government has recently instructed the Department of Culture, Arts and Leisure in Northern Ireland to 'protect, nurture and grow our cultural capital for today and tomorrow, *and thereby make a significant contribution to wider government priorities in health education and the economy'* (emphasis added).[43]

The fact that politicians value the instrumental outcomes of culture has a number of effects:

o   Culture gets partly reconfigured by the instrumental priorities of funding, with resources flowing to support instrumental aims such as economic regeneration.
o   Different funding streams that exist at different political levels – supranational, national, regional, local – often have different and sometimes conflicting priorities, thus creating confusion for professionals.
o   Measurement is needed in order to determine whether instrumental outcomes have been achieved. Money thus flows into measurement, and only those things that can be measured get measured.
o   Culture becomes stuck in 'service agent' mode, expected to achieve extraneous purposes.
o   A focus on instrumental value can detract from intrinsic value.
o   The bureaucracy of instrumental approaches can alienate partners, especially those from the private sector.

5. The mismatch of value concerns

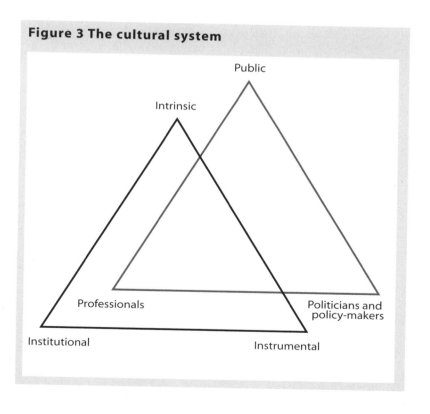

Figure 3 The cultural system

Public

Intrinsic

Professionals

Politicians and
policy-makers

Institutional

Instrumental

Combining the analysis of value as being intrinsic–instrumental–institutional with the contextual schema of public–politician–professional generates insights into where the 'cultural system' is failing either to realise or to articulate value (figure 3). As we have seen, each 'P' places emphasis on different aspects of the 'I' valuation triangle:

- ○ Politicians and policy-makers are primarily concerned with instrumental outcomes.
- ○ Professionals are primarily concerned with intrinsic value.
- ○ The public is primarily concerned with intrinsic and with institutional value.

It is therefore not surprising that much misunderstanding has arisen in the bilateral relationships between these three groups; each conversation is marked either by its absence or its dysfunctionality.

Politicians, policy-makers and professionals

Politicians want measurable, tangible results that help deliver government policy predictably, cost-effectively and on a mass scale, because that is the job of politics. But professionals work in the cultural field first and foremost because of their commitment to intrinsic values.

From the professionals' point of view, the situation in which they find themselves is described by Stuart Davies, the director of the independent charity National Heritage, when he says:

Many museums seem to be under pressure – especially financial and stakeholder pressure. They feel it is increasingly difficult to maintain what has been built up in the late twentieth century in what appears to them to be a much tougher twenty-first century environment and probably getting worse. There is widespread frustration that what they – the people who are running museums – have identified as priority museum needs are apparently often not shared by government, government agencies, or local authorities.[44]

This quotation makes the mismatch of value goals between politicians and professionals crystal clear. The problem is not that museum professionals – or other cultural professionals – do not know the value of what they do. Their sense of vocation tells them that. But those who create the operational context for their work – government, government agencies or local authorities – do not recognise the value. The question then becomes how to create mutual understanding and constructive engagement between these two groups. Two decades of supplying 'evidence' do not appear to have worked, but perhaps if both politicians and professionals understand each other's value positions clearly, and recognise their respective legitimacy and limitations, we may move in the right direction.

This is urgently needed, because the mismatch of value goals, and the consequent misunderstanding between politicians and professionals, has had the following results:

○ The level of direction from government and thereon through the funding chain has increased considerably, suggesting lower levels of trust in professionals on the part of politicians. For example, the ACE *Peer Review* notes: 'Arts Council England believes that DCMS has responded with increased scrutiny and duplication of functions while the DCMS believes that the scrutiny is necessary because it fears that Arts Council England is unlikely to meet some of its targets.'[45]

○ Politics has increasingly seen culture as a deficit model – to cure social ills – rather than, as the professionals see it, a positive pro-social model.

○ Political equivocation about culture has been manifest in stop/go funding for the last 25 years. This is true not only in the UK, where budget settlements have ranged at national and local level from cuts, to standstill to quite large increases, but, according to the US National Endowment for the Arts, is generally true across OECD countries.[46]

○ Professionals have had to make their case to local and national government with depressing frequency and in terms that do not match their own value concerns (and thus appear to them to be empty bureaucratic exercises). John Fox of Welfare State International wrote this valedictory statement:

Walking the tightrope of arts funding between look-at-me celebrity and surrogate social work has become untenable. All our goals of the '60s: access, disability awareness and multicultural participation, have been established but now such agendas come before the art. We joined to make spontaneous playful art outside the ghetto – not to work three years ahead in a goal-oriented corporate institution where matched funding and value-added output tick boxes destroy imaginative excess.[47]

Professionals thus feel unloved, misunderstood and frustrated, and the situation is no better for the politicians. As Tessa Jowell has written:

Too often politicians have been forced to debate culture in terms only of its instrumental benefits to other agendas – education, the reduction of crime, improvements in wellbeing – explaining – or in some instances almost apologising for – our investment in culture only in terms of something else.[48]

Exactly who – HM Treasury? the media? self-censorship? – is forcing politicians to debate culture in this reductive way is an interesting question, but the politicians' sense of frustration is palpable, and Tessa Jowell's response is to make a timely and inspiring plea to her colleagues:

In political and public discourse in this country we have avoided the more difficult approach of investigating, questioning and celebrating what culture actually does in and of itself. There is another story to tell on culture and it's up to politicians in my position to give a lead in changing the atmosphere, and changing the terms of debate.[49]

This leadership is welcome, but it begs the question: how do we go beyond rhetoric? We must do more than 'change the atmosphere'. How can cultural organisations be liberated from PSA targets, service level 'agreements and the language of bureaucracy and shift their compass further, concentrating on giving high-quality cultural experiences to the public?

Politicians, policy-makers and the public

Politicians often talk in terms of delivery. In culture the messages are: free entry to museums, new lottery-funded buildings, more children engaging in culture. These are all significant achievements, but they miss the point. Just as in other areas of public life, such as health and education, what matters most is the public's own assessment of the value that it is getting from what the politicians do. Messages about spending more, increased delivery, outputs and outcomes – that is, about instrumental value – tell us nothing about what the public *itself* values.

For that, we have to look at what citizens themselves say about culture. But because politics has failed to understand the public's concern with intrinsic and institutional value, attempts to uncover what the public values about culture at a mass level (as opposed to customer surveys by individual organisations) have so far been relatively primitive. Fortunately they are beginning to become more sophisticated.

○   Basic surveys of audience numbers and participation
    show levels of *engagement* by different social and ethnic
    groups (see figure 4) in particular areas of cultural life.
    For example, in museums, 28 per cent of school visits to
    museums in all three Renaissance in the Regions hubs

Figure 4 Percentage attending at least one artistic or cultural event in the last 12 months, by ethnic group

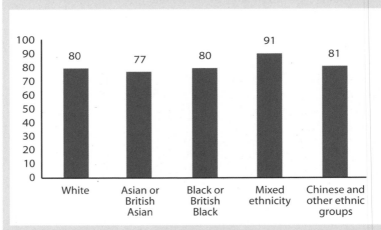

Source: A Bridgwood, *Focus on Cultural Diversity: The arts in England – attendance, participation and attitudes* (London: ACE, UK Film Council and Re:source, 2003)

were made by schools from the 10 per cent most deprived wards in the UK[50] and, where Black, Asian, Chinese mixed and other ethnic groups make up 8.1 per cent of the UK's population aged 12–74, they made up 12.1 per cent of cinema-goers in 2003/04.[51]

In terms of class, a joint survey by Arts Council England and Re:source concluded that:

Taking all types of event together, there was a clear association between socio-economic status and the likelihood of attendance at arts and cultural events. In 2003, the proportions who reported going to at least one event in the year prior to interview in 2003 ranged from 91 per cent of the managerial and professional groups (89 per cent for 2001) to 69 per cent of those in semi-routine and routine occupations (67 per cent for 2001).[52]

Similarly, a 2003 MORI report, *The Impact of Free Entry to Museums*, warned of the nationally funded institutions that, 'while the number of people coming through the door might have dramatically increased, the profile of a typical "population" of museum or gallery visitors has remained relatively stable, and firmly in favour of the "traditional" visitor groups'.[53] There is still a strong bias towards visits by the well educated and affluent, and geographically, by those in the South East of England. People with a degree are almost four times as likely as those with no formal qualifications to have increased their visits as a result of free museum entry.

○   Statistics concerning public *approval* for spending on the arts show a confused picture: general assent, a wish for more local provision, but a high level of indifference (see table 1).[54]

The figures in table 1 suggest that culture shares the same public perception problem as other public services, in particular health. People are generally satisfied with their own local experience of the health service, but more sceptical of the system at a national level.

Statistics about more particular cultural provision show very high levels of approval. According to VisitBritain, six out of the ten most visited attractions in the UK are museums and galleries.[55] According to Arts Council England statistics, visiting a library is second only to film-going in the list of arts activities undertaken.[56] A report published recently by the National Consumer Council (NCC) states that 'investment in museums and galleries has paid off handsomely', and records 95 per cent satisfaction ratings for museums and galleries, the highest for any public service studied.[57]

Table 1 Public approval for spending on the arts

Statement	Much too high or too high (%)	About right (%)	Too low, much too low (%)	Don't know (%)	Base
Arts and culture should receive public funding	79	11	8	2	5974
The amount of public money spent on the arts in my area is ...	9	42	25	24	5976
The amount of public money spent on the arts in this country is ...	21	44	17	18	5976

Source: ACE, *Arts in England 2003: Attendance, participation and attitudes*

O   In *Capturing Cultural Value* it was suggested that techniques of *contingent valuation*, usually applied in environmental and transport economics, could be used to shed light on the public's own assessment of the value it received from culture. A recent survey, *Bolton's Museum, Library and Archive Services: An economic valuation* by Jura Consultants,[58] does exactly that, looking at Use Value, Option Value and Existence Value.[59] The headline conclusion is that Bolton's museum, library and archive service together receives £6.5 million of public funding, while the public values them at £10.4 million (£7.4 million by users and, crucially, £3 million by non-users).

The British Library has also done a contingent valuation study, and an as yet unpublished Australian survey has produced similar results to those found in Bolton.

○ The Heritage Lottery Fund has convened *citizens' juries* to articulate what it is about heritage that the public values. Although the sample sizes are small, results show an unprompted high level of sophistication on the part of the public, and an appreciation of what culture can and does achieve, once they are made aware of the provision.

If politics is to understand why the general public (which embraces those who do not participate in culture as well as those who do) values public spending on culture, these techniques of contingent valuation and opinion research need to become much more widespread. Interestingly, these early studies suggest that citizens value their cultural life and cultural facilities more than politicians think they do. The overall pattern then is encouraging: high levels of approval for public funding; culture valued at more than spend; a sophisticated and improving public understanding of culture. Certainly there is plenty of work to be done in making culture available to all on an equal basis, but the tide is flowing: the public are increasingly aware of, interested in and capable of shaping their own culture; it is up to the professionals to harness the power of the public will in pursuit of the public good.

Professionals and the public

One might expect there to be a natural alliance between the public and the professionals when it comes to cultural value because both are mainly concerned with intrinsic value. But the relationship is not straightforward: a tension exists that is sometimes constructive and sometimes destructive. This should not cause surprise. In every sphere the expert by definition will be operating at a level of greater sophistication and depth than the laity. But in every sphere that relationship is being renegotiated. In science, for example, the unquestioning acceptance of expert opinion is a thing of the past, and there are currently hot debates about the public understanding of, and agenda-setting in, science.[60]

The age of deference may be over, but that does not mean that the public has ceased to be interested in expertise. On the contrary, serious investigations of art, heritage, culture and history draw large audiences on television.[61] Professionals have a role as educators and arbiters, but also as guardians. It is their job to ensure intergenerational equity and the maintenance of the cultural ecology – a job that on the surface can conflict with the short-term public will as expressed by the media (see chapter 6). Professionals also have a legitimate role in shaping public opinion and encouraging and validating public debate. An example of how this can work in practice is given in chapter 8.

In the cultural world, the undermining of respect for the role of expert opinion has been lamented as 'dumbing down', but it is wrong to think that increased participation in, and enjoyment of, culture must be at the expense of quality. Such a view is patronising to the public and does not accord with the reality of a public that is becoming better educated, more aspirational and more discriminating. Far from being a zero sum game, culture is a sphere of infinitely expanding possibilities.

Professionals and the public have an interest in the best and not the worst intrinsic value; they should be natural allies against the dominance of instrumental values in culture. But over the last two decades professionals have, naturally enough, prioritised establishing legitimacy with their funders over making their case with the public. 'Advocacy' has meant producing 'good stories' and 'convincing numbers' to make the case for next year's grant, rather than building a broad basis of popular support. Competing for limited resources, cultural professionals have concentrated on arguing on behalf of their own institutions, or sometimes for their specialist artform. This struggle for funding priority between different parts of the cultural sector has been demeaning and counterproductive, and has done nothing to build broad public support for an increase in what is, in national terms, a very small budget.

For the cultural professionals, the public represents a source of vast potential in the fight to establish political and financial support: more people engage with the arts than vote – in the 2005 general election, 61.5 per cent of the electorate voted;[62] ACE, by contrast, can point to some 80 per cent attending at least one arts event in 2003.[63] But beyond that, only public support can provide the legitimacy for politics to fund culture.

Statistics about public support and contingent valuation should make professionals more confident in their engagement with the public. They must stop thinking of citizens only as 'audiences' or 'potential audiences'; even at their most passive, the public are involved in creative engagements with culture.

Professionals need to seek new ways to engage with the public, but they also need to look to the politicians. Part of the problem in the public–professional relationship is that professionals tend to focus on supply-side solutions, because that is the area where they exercise greatest influence. For example, within the cultural sector, some organisations worry about the demographics of their audience base, and then do what they can to change it with programming, ticket prices, arranging transport, and 'outreach' programmes. But the fundamental issue lies on the demand side. Numerous international studies have shown a strong correlation between attendance at cultural events on the one hand, and levels of education, familiarity and socialisation with culture on the other (in other words, if your parents took you to the theatre, the habit tends to stick).[64] The message is clear: increasing audiences for the future will depend as much and probably more on what happens in the education system and in town centres than on the pricing policies of museums, galleries and theatres. Professionals need to make themselves heard in planning committees and in local education authorities. Which takes us full circle to where this section started – with politics.

6. The role of the media

The relationship between the public, politicians and professionals is reflected in and partly formed by the print and broadcast media (figure 5).

The media discourse about culture is grouped around a number of themes, creating a paradoxical picture in which the media both support and attack art and artists:

- There is extensive daily, and particularly weekend, coverage of cultural events. Critical comment is thoughtful, well informed and regular. Commercial media commit the resources that they do because large numbers of their readers, listeners and viewers are interested (this is another reason why cultural professionals should be optimistic). In the broadsheets and parts of the broadcast media, this approach extends more widely to cultural policy and cultural politics as well as events. But when the arts become 'news' the reporting almost always becomes negative.
- In the tabloids, there is consistent antagonism to culture, some of it based on inaccurate reporting. Recent examples include an attack on money invested or, as the *Sun* put it, 'lavished' and 'blown' on art in hospitals. This was a classic case of trumped-up outrage because, as the paper

Figure 5 Interest groups and the media

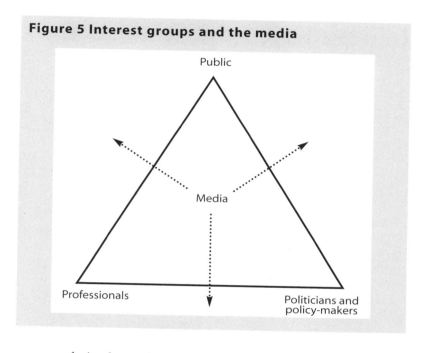

admitted, practically all of the money came from charitable sources, not from the public purse. Interestingly, a politician was on hand to knock art: 'Tory health spokesman Tim Loughton said the spree would infuriate patients and taxpayers.'[65] The instrumental argument that health outcomes are improved by art in hospitals was ignored, in spite of the fact that, according to Dr Richard Smith, editor of the *British Medical Journal*, 'diverting 0.5 per cent of the healthcare budget to the arts would improve the health of people in Britain'.[66]

○ Another recent example of hostility to culture was the media reaction to Addenbrooke's Hospital advertising to recruit an art curator 'on a salary of nearly £37,000 a year'.[67] Again, the funding came not from public sources but from charities, and did not affect health spending budgets at all. The case was reported on the front page of London's daily free paper *Metro*.

O Tabloid newspapers glory in what an earlier age would have called philistinism, on the assumption that this reflects the views of their readers. This comment from the *Daily Mail* on the Momart fire that destroyed a large number of twentieth-century works is typical: 'Didn't millions cheer as this "rubbish" went up in flames?'[68]

O While attacking art and culture, many newspapers simultaneously worry that the nation is 'dumbing down'.[69]

These observations are not meant to serve as media-bashing. Blaming the media is an all too common aspect of the 'cultural whinge'.[70] In many ways the media play a constructive role: they are part of a wider culture that has produced a nation that thrives on book-buying, the visual arts and music. But tabloid negativity does contribute to the production of a political class that avoids public association with culture. This in turn has created difficulties for cultural policy, with politicians tip-toeing around cultural issues. In this regard the public comments of Kim Howells about the Turner Prize in 2002, where he dismissed the entries as 'cold, mechanical conceptual bullshit', should be welcomed: however basic and tabloid-friendly they may have been, at least he voiced his opinions about the quality of the work.[71]

The tabloid assault on the arts has unfortunate repercussions not just for cultural organisations, but directly for artists, as this story from the *Guardian* about the sculptor Rachel Whiteread demonstrates:

> *The maker of* House *and the* Holocaust Memorial . . . *speaks as someone who has been through the wringer of public controversy. In the weeks leading up to the unveiling of her Turbine Hall installation she has been desperate to avoid cooked-up tabloid outrage of the kind that led to Andre's bricks being doused with blue vegetable dye.*[72]

In some ways culture offers an easy target for lazy journalists, but two points are worth noting if things are to change.

The first is that the cultural sector itself needs to find public defenders: the field is often left wide open, with no challenge made to inaccurate reporting or idiotic commentary. The second is that the press, and politicians, are now finding themselves caught off-balance by a public that is more sympathetic to contemporary culture. When the decision was announced in March 2005 to commission Marc Quinn's sculpture *Alison Lapper Pregnant* for the Fourth Plinth in Trafalgar Square, press and politicians were divided: the *Sun*'s headline was 'Travulga Square',[73] and a spokesperson for the Conservative Party said that 'the politically correct lobby has prevailed. Whilst childbirth is a great thing to celebrate, I still think we should have focused on individuals of great achievement the nation ought to commemorate.'[74] The *Daily Mail*'s opinion was that 'a vast majority of people would have liked to have seen a statue of an iconic . . . role model, with the Queen Mother the favourite.'[75] But within 24 hours it became apparent that public opinion was strongly, if not universally, in favour of the sculpture. The public admired Alison Lapper, a severely disabled woman who had overcome immense difficulties to become an artist and a mother. The *Sun* quickly changed its tune and next day ran an article entitled 'Amazing Alison'.[76]

This is not an isolated case – Tate Modern and Antony Gormley's *Angel of the North* both received initial negative press comment, and they are now national and regional icons. With a public that is becoming better educated, more confident in its relationship with 'high culture' (because of its increasing dovetailing with popular culture), and more participative, the tabloid attacks on culture, such as the annual posturing around the Turner Prize, may start to look old-fashioned, out of touch and foolish.

7. Research, evidence and advocacy

What is research for?

A huge amount of time, effort, energy and money has been devoted to the gathering of evidence about culture over the past two decades (figure 6). The total cost of all the research and evaluation that has been done, and the proportion of the cultural spend devoted to these tasks, are unknown, but it is certainly the case that cultural professionals take research very seriously, even when the amount of public money involved in the relevant cultural enterprise is small. Why is research undertaken? There are four reasons why it *could* be undertaken:

○ to generate information from which individuals and organisations can learn
○ to generate or synthesise information on which policy and funding decisions can be based
○ to provide the raw material for advocacy
○ to fulfil bureaucratic demands.

These purposes are often confused, which is one reason why so much research is discredited.[77] For example, the recent *Peer Review* of Arts Council England calls for ACE to be 'the first port of call for anyone . . . seeking reliable information about the arts' but also to be 'a more effective advocate for the arts . . . clearly demonstrating their impact back to government.'[78] These two aims – objective information and

Figure 6 Information flow

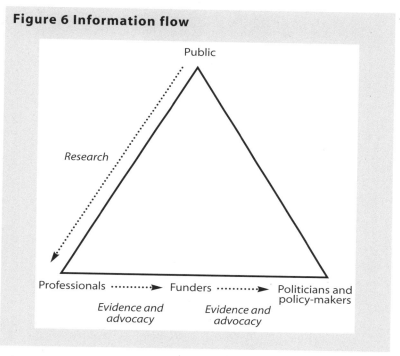

advocacy – are in large part congruent, but they may also conflict, not in the sense that advocacy requires or uses inaccurate information, but in the sense that advocacy suppresses the negative and accentuates the positive, and is therefore selective in its use of information.

The problems with research

In addition to the problems with research mentioned in the section 'Instrumental value' in chapter 3, the following factors need to be considered:

○ Measurement tends to occur where it is easiest, not necessarily where it is most useful.

○ As Kate Oakley has commented, 'there is far less research

at the "consumption" end of the cycle such as exhibition and reception than at the "production" end.'[79] In other words, the activity of cultural professionals is measured much more than the public response to it. This reflects the cultural system's introversion, and the priority given to the professional/politics nexus.

○ Although consistent longitudinal evidence is rare, it is not necessarily always to be encouraged because fixed, consistent systems of data collection conflict with the essential dynamism and exploration of cultural practice.

○ Data-gathering often fails to capture value, because it is concerned not with subjective responses but with objective outcomes.

○ Professionals often do not know why they are asked to produce evidence. Very little feedback is given to them about how the information that they have supplied is used.

○ Organisations are often ill-equipped to act on the evidence that research provides. This is particularly true where evidence is gathered for advocacy, but where the structures and relationships to make that advocacy effective are missing.

○ Evidence is gathered and used almost exclusively in a conversation where professionals respond to the demands of politics, or where they try to use evidence as an advocacy tool in their relationship with politicians. However, politicians appear to distrust the evidence: in England, the Arts Council grant has been frozen. Would that have happened if the Treasury had been convinced by the mass of data adduced about the social and economic utility of the arts?

There are two schools of thought about the need for an evidence base in the funding argument for culture. There are those who think that all that is needed is to 'get it right' – if cultural professionals produce enough rigorous data conclusively proving the links between public investment in culture and its economic return then the funding argument will be won. Whether or not such an impregnable case can be made is an open question, but leaving that aside there are others who believe that data alone will never shift political thinking, that hearts need to be persuaded as well as minds.

I favour the latter view. I am not arguing against rigorous data – of course research should be as methodologically sound as possible – but the idea that rational argument always works is naïve. Evidence has to be thorough, but it has to be met by receptivity, and that is often a matter of emotional response and worldview. When Margaret Thatcher's economic adviser Sir Alan Peacock was told the value of the creative industries his response was 'I don't believe it.'[80] It is unclear whether he meant that the data were flawed or whether he did not want to be persuaded, but the use of the word 'believe' is telling. In any event, rational argument only gets you so far. Neither Labour's creation of an arts minister in the 1960s nor the spending cuts imposed by the Conservatives in the 1980s were based on hard evidence; they happened because the politicians of the day had differing ideas about the function of the state and the role of culture in public life.

More research?

Many studies have called for more and better research.[81] This appeal needs to be interrogated. Data-gathering can all too easily become an end in itself, a case of displacement activity, or a means to postpone decisions until there is solid evidence – which is never quite solid enough. Furthermore we need to know why we want more research. Data is useful only if it can be turned into knowledge, so we should decide what constitutes the right sort and quantity of data, and to what use it will be put, and by whom, before asking for more. On top of that, unless the right organisational structures and attitudes are in place to act on what we can learn from the data, then much research will be a waste of time. If organisations do not have the capacity to adapt, targeting-setting simply sets up failure. Yet these questions are not being properly interrogated – there exists a general assumption that more means better.

A new regime for research

A new regime for research and evidence-gathering is needed to overcome the current confusion. Such a regime would have at its heart the following principles:

○ *Clarity of purpose.* Research projects would not simply ask what do we want to know, but why do we want to know it, and what will we do with the knowledge. Who will gain from this research, and how will it be used?

○ *Cost-effectiveness.* In a world of resource constraints, we should interrogate the cost of research in proportion to the rest of the cultural spend. This applies at individual project and organisation level, as well as on a local, regional and national scale. Have we got the balance right between counting trees and planting them? Given the small sums of money spent by government on culture, why does politics require so much effort to go into proving the worth of the spend?

○ *Research questions should be set by the learner.* Research findings are of most use when the questions being asked are formulated by the people who will use the answers. In the cultural world many organisations have research tasks, methodologies and agendas set for them by funders. Moving to learner-centred research will involve cultural organisations seeking help with setting the terms of research.

○ *Feedback.* When information is gathered, the use to which it has been put should be communicated to those who have been required to provide it.

○ *Taking action.* More thought should be given to the receptive capacity of organisations to act on research findings.

○ *Taking the public into account.* More effort should be put
   into researching the consumption of culture – in
   particular, the public's views, responses and satisfaction.
   This will entail more contingent valuation studies, more
   opinion seeking and more observational research.
○ *Investigating the intrinsic.* There should be more
   articulation of issues of quality.[82]

All the above suggests that funders should change the basis of
research. Most research is commissioned by funders or demanded by
them as a grant condition. When funders set the terms of research it is
generally of more use to them than to the organisation concerned.
Funders should instead:

○ Require organisations to adopt practices of reflective
   learning. Organisations should be allowed to decide for
   themselves what information they need, and how to
   gather it, in order to improve their own performance.
   They can then demonstrate to funders how improvements
   have been generated, and both organisations and funders
   can share that learning.
○ Make clear what information they need for their own
   learning and policy decision-making. Professionals are
   often confused about why they are being asked for
   information; they should be told why, and shown how
   their information gathering has been of use to the funder.
○ Pay more attention to gathering information for use in
   advocacy and engagement with the public, rather than
   being (as at present) used almost exclusively between
   politicians and professionals.

8. Developing a new legitimacy

An end to introversion

Understanding the different types of value that culture creates, and understanding what is important to politicians, the public and cultural professionals, helps clarify where misunderstandings are occurring. The interest of politicians in instrumental value has dominated over the last 25 years. It is understandable, and is an important feature of the value of culture. But recently the dominance of that perspective has been questioned, with more recognition given to the importance of intrinsic values. In essence, this debate about values has been an attempt to improve the terms of engagement between politicians and professionals, but what has been missing so far is the voice of the public. Now, cultural professionals need to engage more, and differently, with the public in order to merit a broad-based democratic mandate.

The 'cultural system' has become a closed conversation between professionals and politicians, with too much emphasis placed on satisfying funders, rather than on achieving the self-generated purposes of the cultural organisations themselves, or on engaging the public. Professionals talk among themselves, and talk to funders, but rarely talk to the public about what they do. Consequently the public has little idea about how culture operates and what it's capable of doing.

Compare and contrast the way that a private sector company deals with the public with the way in which a major cultural organisation does this. Both have an everyday face, where what they do – say selling clothes and putting on concerts – is perfectly obvious to the public. Both have websites, customer care training programmes, complaints procedures and so on. But once a year the company will release its annual report to the press; it will hold a meeting of its shareholders; it will explain its business and what it intends to do in the future, and its board of directors will be subject to questioning. The shareholders will vote for who they want as directors.

The cultural organisation will not have a public meeting (except in rare cases); the annual report will be sent to funders and a few others; the public will not see, or question, the board of trustees, and usually will not know who they are, nor how they were appointed. The cultural organisation will not discuss its future plans, and the public will have little idea about the organisation's potential, its limitations, its financial situation, its governance, or its staffing structure. The public will probably have only a hazy idea of who owns it (the council? a trust? an individual?), and whether it is commercial or charitable. In these circumstances it is hardly surprising that culture can often seem to the public to be an esoteric recipient of 'subsidy'.

Engaging with the public

Public accountability is best achieved directly with the public – and it is not adequately provided by outmoded and creaking systems of governance (that are in any case ripe for reform), nor by reporting lines to funders. But accountability is an enfeebled notion, a mere baseline for the relationship that could exist between culture and the public. A much richer dialogue is needed, but there are barriers to its creation:

O   Most of the introverted conversation among
      professionals, and between professionals and politicians,
      uses a language that means little to the public. Even this
      pamphlet, while seeking to remedy the situation, will, by

its context, fall into the same category. But the concept of 'cultural value' *does* provide a new way of thinking about the public voice and finding ways to encourage its expression. One step must certainly be to scrutinise the language of public policy closely, and to abandon, or explain, cultural jargon when communicating with the public.

O   From the public's point of view the cultural sector lacks coherence. The sector contains few people who speak on behalf of the complete cultural world and who are as comfortable talking about a library as a theatre. This has come about partly through cultural subsectors needing to defend their own turf in the face of inadequate funding and partly from a professional caution about speaking on someone else's behalf, but looked at from the outside, culture consists of many interest groups, such as those for the arts, or museums, or the visual arts, all pulling in subtly different directions. Unlike the business world there is no Institute of Cultural Directors or Confederation of British Culture to provide a voice for the whole of culture outside government – a place where leaders can provide media input, and give media reaction. If public engagement is to increase it needs to take place on many levels and in many contexts. As well as individual institutions and cultural groupings such as 'heritage' and 'dance', we need the sector as a whole to have a voice, and to provide a forum where the public can interact.

Professionals will gain greater legitimacy and support for what they do if they engage more with the public in order to understand public needs and desires and to create value for the public. They need to find new ways for the public to generate preferences. There are already many examples, such as:

O   egg in Bath, the Unicorn Theatre in London and

Bournemouth Library, all of which 'involved the client' in the design of their buildings

○ The Sage Gateshead, which engages with a wide public in new ways: 'The opening . . . did not take the form of the usual gala concert with a VIP guest list, but instead offered an intensively programmed open weekend (for) 15,000 attendees'[83]

○ the Heritage Lottery Fund, which has created citizens' juries to understand why the public values heritage

○ Nottingham Playhouse, which set up a weblog to explain the working processes behind one of their productions[84]

○ weblogs to encourage audience involvement and critical response. An internet search reveals that very few cultural organisations have set up their own blogs.

9. Conclusion

The foregoing analysis challenges current practice and policy, and suggests several prescriptions for change. At a fundamental level it argues that the traditional approaches to setting policy goals, and funding the arts and culture, will never succeed in creating the deeper legitimacy that is required if the aspirations of professionals and politicians, and the full potential of public involvement, are to be made real.

My argument is that such legitimacy is a precondition for securing a larger, and more secure, place for culture in our wider public life, and therefore in the priorities of democratically elected governments. Creating such legitimacy will depend on institutional innovation that engages the public in understanding and contributing to the creation of cultural value. Encouraging such innovation by the full range of institutions and practitioners should be the principal aim of any structural reform of arts funding and policy.

The strategic reform that is needed should not be contemplated without simultaneously addressing the kinds of understanding, learning and development that are necessary for cultural professionals fully to meet the challenge that I have laid out, of engaging more, and more directly, with the public. This is because solutions are best generated by people who are closest to the issues, rather than by outside commentators – especially in a field such as culture, where we are dealing with dynamic relationships and not timeless 'facts'.

The 'cultural value' framework helps people and organisations to understand themselves, articulate their purposes, and make decisions, because it provides:

- a language to talk about why the public values culture
- a more democratic approach, offering the opportunity to build wider legitimacy for public funding
- the opportunity to ease adaptation to a more participative model of culture
- a reassertion of the role of the professional practitioner
- a rationale for why the funding system should be less directive
- a means by which politicians and professionals can understand each other's positions, leading to improved relationships and a better concordat with the public.

One advantage of the analysis is that it recognises tensions and complexities without seeking to resolve all of them, because some of them are unresolvable. The approach of the funding system and of political rhetoric has been to keep these tensions hidden, but they need to be acknowledged. The artistic director's wish to do challenging new work, the politician's desire to see a more diverse audience and the public's conservatism need to be understood and accommodated (particularly at the systemic level rather than at the level of a single production) rather than fudged or, worse, ignored. The approach to value shown by the Arizona Commission for the Arts articulates just such an accommodation:

> It is not expected that every project the Commission funds or undertakes will serve the entire public, nor must every grant or project deliver broad and general public value. Some projects are narrow, deep and specific; some don't focus on a public event, but make possible the creation of work that adds to the artistic canon. These are no more or less valuable than those that serve a large number of people.[85]

'Cultural value' identifies fundamental problems in the current approach to publicly funded culture, but there are reasons for optimism, because some of the changes that are needed could come about in the context of current policy concerns such as:

O   governance reform, which should seek a better understanding of institutional value, of cultural engagement and learning, and of professional innovation

O   investment in leadership, which can help professionals understand their role in creating cultural value

O   value measurement and articulation, which is increasingly recognising the multiplicity of values that culture creates, and beginning to show how much the public does in fact value culture

O   the government's well-being and respect agendas, which recognise that many social problems are small-c cultural problems

O   issues of national, regional, local and personal identity, where the construction, reflection and expression of identity are recognised as cultural phenomena.

But these opportunities could be lost if they simply replicate traditional approaches; and on top of that, more should be done:

O   National policy should be clearer and braver about setting the terms of its cultural objectives, and clarifying the right of citizens to be enthused and delighted by culture – a right that is explicit in Article 27 (1) of the United Nations' Universal Declaration of Human Rights: 'Everyone has the right freely to participate in the cultural life of the community, to enjoy the arts, and to share in scientific advancement and its benefits.'[86]

O   Politicians should show more leadership in their engagement and enjoyment of culture. They should be seen at performances, express their preferences, and talk to the media about their enthusiasms. Perhaps, like the French, we will one day have a prime minister who is a serious, published poet.

○ There should be a new statutory obligation for local authorities to invest in the creation of cultural value, unconstrained by numerical definitions or the need to address other priorities of local government. There is here both a big opportunity and a very real threat to cultural services if this is not done.

○ Regional policy needs to lose its obsession with economic development and to encompass a much broader set of concerns, making culture both a primary building block and an expression of regional identity, prosperity and well-being.

○ More explicit 'risk capital' is needed in culture, not only for cultural production but for institutional innovation. Culture is a place where innovation comes with the territory, and therefore a sphere that can develop models for other parts of civil society.

○ A new research and development agenda is needed that capitalises on the growing interest in cultural value. One aspect of such a new regime would be to focus on issues of organisational capacity for change, as much as on the outputs and outcomes of cultural endeavour. Another would be to develop new surveys, datasets and qualitative evaluations that seek to understand public experience.

If the public funding of culture is to rest on firm foundations there must be a proper recognition of the value concerns of everyone involved. An accommodation must be found through informed debate. An over-reliance on any one element of the I–I–I value triangle (see figure 1), or an overemphasis on the concerns of any of the P–P–P interest groups (see figure 2), is detrimental to a properly functioning cultural system. Like the US constitution, a balance of power is needed.

An example of such a balance can be found in the recent case of the sculpture erected on Trafalgar Square's Fourth Plinth: *Alison Lapper Pregnant*, referred to in chapter 6. The process that preceded the unveiling is an interesting one. Six artists were chosen by an expert commission to put forward proposals. The maquettes of their ideas were shown in the National Gallery and on a website, and the public were invited to comment but not to vote. The expert commission then made a recommendation to the Mayor of London, whose final decision it was to pay for and erect this particular sculpture, subject to further local scrutiny via the planning process. Since its unveiling the statue has done what a public artwork should do: it has excited debate, raised all sorts of questions about the place of art in our lives, the nature of public space, and issues of taste.

This example shows a balance being struck between the public will, professional expertise and political interest. The public was given a voice, but not a vote – instead, professional expertise came into play right at the start, and in the form of a recommendation by the commissioning group. But the final decisions were rightly made by politicians, because public money was being spent, and public space was affected: democratic accountability ultimately lies in the realm of politics.

This healthy relationship between the public, professionals and politicians offered, as we have seen in chapter 6, a challenge to the media. Partly because of the process that was followed the public does not just value *Alison Lapper Pregnant*, they treasure her. That is a demonstration of public legitimacy, and when that happens the nervousness shown by politicians, the hesitancy of cultural professionals, and the negativity of the media all disappear.

Notes

1   See, for instance, P Kelly, 'Defending the arts budget', *Arts Professional*, 19 Dec 2005.

2   'Arts Council England and DCMS must work together to rebuild mutual trust, and to cement crucial working relationships at both the strategic and operational levels', Arts Council England and Department for Culture, Media and Sport, *Arts Council England: Report of the Peer Review* (London: ACE and DCMS, 2005).

3   For discussion of such bad publicity, see C Higgins, 'The final act: English National Opera chief quits and blames "persistent hostility"', *Guardian*, 22 Dec 2005; see www.guardian.co.uk/arts/news/story/0,11711,1672411,00.html (accessed 11 Jan 2006).

4   See R Williams, *Keywords* (New York: Oxford University Press, 1983, rev. edn); see excerpt at http://pubpages.unh.edu/~dml3/880williams.htm#N_1_ (accessed 5 Feb 2006).

5   See www.culture.gov.uk/about_dcms/QuickLinks/f_a_q/ faq_definition_of_culture.htm?properties=%2C%2Fabout_dcms%2FQuickLin ks%2Ff_a_q%2Fdefault%2C&month= (accessed 11 Jan 2006).

6   Department for Culture, Media and Sport, *DCMS Evidence Toolkit* (formerly, The Regional Cultural Data Framework) (London: DCMS, 2005).

7   For further details, see www.demos.co.uk/catalogue/valuingculturespeeches/ (accessed 4 Feb 2006).

8   T Jowell, *Government and the Value of Culture* (London: DCMS, 2004).

9   J Holden, *Capturing Cultural Value: How culture has become a tool of government policy* (London: Demos, 2004).

10 See www.arts.gov/pub/Notes/74.pdf (accessed 11 Jan 2006).

11 Holden, *Capturing Cultural Value*.

12 K McCarthy et al, *Gifts of the Muse: Reframing the debate about the benefits of the arts* (Santa Monica: RAND Corporation, 2004).

13 M Boehm, 'Arts funding report sparks controversy', *Los Angeles Times*, 16 Feb

2005.

14   R Hewison and J Holden, *Challenge and Change: HLF and cultural value* (London: Heritage Lottery Fund and Demos, 2004); and D Throsby, *Economics and Culture* (Cambridge: Cambridge University Press, 2002).

15   See Holden *Capturing Cultural Value*; S Selwood, 'The politics of data collection', *Cultural Trends* 47 (2002); A Ellis, his speech at the Valuing Culture conference, available for download at www.demos.co.uk/catalogue/ valuingculturespeeches/ (accessed 4 Feb 2006); K Oakley, 'Developing the evidence base for support of cultural and creative activities in the South East', South East England Development Agency, 2004; McCarthy, *Gifts of the Muse* (RAND report); DCMS, *DCMS Evidence Toolkit*; and J Carey, *What Good are the Arts?* (London, Faber and Faber, 2005).

16   Arts Council England, *Local Government and the Arts: A vision for partnership*, (London, ACE, 2003), available at www.artscouncil.org.uk/documents/ publications/localgovernmentarts_phpR4yzlj.pdf (accessed 11 Jan 2006).

17   M Moore, *Creating Public Value* (Cambridge MA: Harvard University Press, 1995).

18   See the BBC publication, *Building Public Value*, available at www.bbc.co.uk/thefuture/bpv/prologue.shtml (accessed 11 Jan 2006).

19   See R Hewison and J Holden, *The Right to Art* (London: Demos, 2004), available at www.demos.co.uk/catalogue/righttoartreport/ (accessed 4 Feb 2006); and J Holden and S Jones, *Hitting the Right Note: Learning and participation at The Sage Gateshead* (London: DfES Publication, 2005).

20   Morton Smyth, *Not for the Likes of You: How to reach a broader audience* (Edinburgh: Morton Smyth Ltd, 2004), available at www.mortonsmyth.com (accessed 12 Jan 2006).

21   *Help for the Arts: Report of the Bridges Committee* (London: Calouste Gulbenkian Foundation, 1959).

22   H Wilson, white paper, *Policy for the Arts: The first steps* (London: HMSO, 1965).

23   For fuller expressions of this, see Holden, *Capturing Cultural Value*; McCarthy et al, *Gifts of the Muse*; and Jowell, *Government and the Value of Culture*.

24   ACE and DCMS, *Arts Council England: Report of the Peer Review*.

25   ACE, *Towards 2010: New times, new challenges for the arts* (London: ACE, 2000).

26   See Hewison and Holden, *The Right to Art*, referencing P Bourdieu, *Distinction: A social critique of the judgment of taste*, tr R Nice (London: Routledge, 1984).

27   For more details on Pro-Ams, see C Leadbeater and P Miller, *The Pro-Am Revolution: How enthusiasts are changing our economy and society* (London: Demos, 2004).

28   For example, at the Natural History Museum: for more details see R Ellis et al, *Nature: Who knows?* (London: English Nature Publication, 2005).

29   'Who am I?' is the name of an exhibit that, at the time of writing, is on permanent display at the Science Museum, London.

30   McCarthy et al, *Gifts of the Muse*.

31   M Mean and C Tims, *In Concert* (London: Demos, 2005), available at

www.demos.co.uk/projects/currentprojects/InConcert/ (accessed 4 Feb 2006).

32   For examples of this, see 'There be monsters' at the National Archives, as described in National Archives, *There be Monsters: A case study* (London: National Archives Report, 2005); or literary groups at Deerholt Young Offenders Institute, see Carey, *What Good are the Arts?*

33   A Artner, 'James Cuno: keeping art essential', *Chicago Tribune,* 12 Sep 2004.

34   N Hytner, 'To hell with targets', *Observer,* 12 Jan 2003; available at http://observer.guardian.co.uk/review/story/0,6903,872985,00.html (accessed 11 Jan 2006).

35   See www.mori.com/polls/2005/mpm050523.shtml (accessed 7 Feb 2006).

36   For more details, see *70 Cents for Culture!,* at www.eurocult.org/ (accessed 12 Jan 2006).

37   See www.artscouncil.org.uk/pressnews/ press_detail.php?browse=recent&id=415 (accessed 11 Jan 2006).

38   See www.parliament.uk/parliamentary_committees/ committee_of_public_accounts/pac211004_pn43.cfm (accessed 11 Jan 2006).

39   See www.hm-treasury.gov.uk (accessed 4 Feb 2006).

40   P Kelly, 'Defending the arts budget', *Arts Professional,* 19 Dec 2005.

41   R Eyre, 'Ballot-box blues', *Guardian,* 26 Mar 2005; available at http://books.guardian.co.uk/review/story/0,12084,1445159,00.html (accessed 11 Jan 2006).

42   For fuller discussion, see Holden, *Capturing Cultural Value*; McCarthy et al, *Gifts of the Muse*; and Selwood, 'The politics of data collection'.

43   'Northern Irish arts sidelined', *Arts Professional* 110, 21 Nov 2005.

44   This is quoted on National Heritage's website, www.nationalheritage.org.uk/survey_body.htm (accessed 12 Jan 2006).

45   ACE and DCMS, *Arts Council England: Report of the Peer Review.*

46   See www.arts.gov/pub/Notes/74.pdf (accessed 11 Jan 2006).

47   J Fox, 'Whose culture?', *Arts Professional* 106, 26 Sep 2005.

48   Jowell, *Government and the Value of Culture.*

49   Ibid.

50   E Hooper-Greenhill et al, *What did you Learn at the Museum Today?* (Leicester: Leicester University Press, 2004).

51   UK Film Council, *Statistical Yearbook: Annual review 2003/04* (London: UK Film Council, 2004).

52   See C Fenn et al, *Arts in England 2003: Attendance, participation and attitudes* (London: ACE, 2004); available at www.artscouncil.org.uk/documents/ publications/artsinengland2003_phpkIxL2w.pdf (accessed 4 Feb 2006).

53   A Martin, *The Impact of Free Entry to Museums* (London: MORI, 2003).

54   See www.artscouncil.org.uk/documents/publications/ artsinengland2003_phpkIxL2w.pdf (accessed 4 Feb 2006).

55   VisitBritain, *Visitor Attractions in England 2004* (London: VisitBritain, 2005).

56   Fenn et al, *Arts in England 2003.*

57   E Mayo, *A Playlist for Public Services* (London: National Consumer Council, 2005).

58   Jura Consultants, *Bolton's Museum, Library and Archive Services: An economic valuation* (Edinburgh: Jura Consultants, 2005).

59   For further explanation, see Holden, *Capturing Cultural Value.*

60   See J Wilsdon and R Willis, *See-through Science: Why public engagement needs to move upstream* (London: Demos, 2004); and J Wilsdon, B Wynne and J Stilgoe, *The Public Value of Science: Or how to ensure that science really matters* (London: Demos, 2005).

61   See various entries at www.bbc.co.uk/pressoffice/pressreleases/ (accessed 30 Jan 2006).

62   See www.parliament.uk/commons/lib/research/rp2005/rp05-033.pdf (accessed 11 Jan 2006).

63   Fenn et al, *Arts in England 2003.*

64   See Hewison and Holden, *The Right to Art.*

65   That day's page 3 caption read: 'Stunning Keely, 19, from Kent, was disgusted to learn that nearly £9 million had been blown on art in hospitals. She said "it should be spent on medical equipment and doctors, not on pointless sculptures."' *Sun*, 26 Oct 2005.

66   Quoted in the Campaign for Learning through Museums and Galleries, *Museums of the Mind: Mental health, emotional well-being . . . and museums* (Bude: clmg, 2005).

67   BBC news 3 Aug 2005, see http://news.bbc.co.uk/1/hi/england/cambridgeshire/4732481.stm (accessed 11 Jan 2006).

68   Quoted in D Aaranovitch, 'Ashes to ashes', *Observer*, 30 May 2005, see www.guardian.co.uk/arts/britartfire/story/0,14634,1228015,00.html (accessed 11 Jan 2006).

69   For more details of 'dumbing down', see I Mosley (ed), *Dumbing Down: Culture, politics and the mass media* (Thorverton, Imprint Academic, 2000).

70   The term 'cultural whinge' is David Cannadine's: www.chass.org.au/news/items/020905.pdf (accessed 4 Feb 2006).

71   See http://news.bbc.co.uk/1/hi/uk_politics/2380499.stm (accessed 11 Jan 2006).

72   G Burn, 'Still breaking the mould', *Guardian G2*, 11 Oct 2005, available online at www.guardian.co.uk/arts/features/story/0,11710,1589344,00.html (accessed 4 Feb 2006).

73   *Sun*,16 Mar 2005.

74   Julie Kirkbride MP, quoted in the *Daily Mail*, 16 Mar 2005.

75   Ibid.

76   *Sun*, 18 Mar 2005.

77   'Until the collection and analysis of data is carried out more accurately and objectively, and until the evidence gathered is used more constructively, it could be argued that much data gathering in the cultural sector has been a spurious exercise.' Selwood, 'The politics of data collection'.

78   ACE and DCMS, *Arts Council England: Report of the Peer Review.*

79   K Oakley, 'Developing the evidence base for support of cultural and creative activities in South East England', report to the South East England Development Agency, 2004.

80   Interview for BBC Radio 4's *The Cultural State*, broadcast 23 Sep 2004.
81   For example, Culture South West, 'Joining the dots: cultural sector research in the South West of England', Culture South West report, 2003; Oakley, 'Developing the Evidence Base for Support of Cultural and Creative Activities in the South East'; and DCMS, *DCMS Evidence Toolkit*.
82   Holden, *Capturing Cultural Value*, see chapter 5.
83   Living North and The Sage Gateshead, *The Sage Gateshead: The opening year* (Newcastle: The Sage Gateshead, 2005).
84   See www.nottinghamplayhouse.co.uk/index.cfm/page/content.index.cfm/cid/220/navid/67/parentid/39 (accessed 4 Feb 2006).
85   Arizona Commission for the Arts, *Creating Public Value*, (Phoenix, AZ: ACA, 2004).
86   See: www.un.org/Overview/rights.html (accessed 5 Feb 2006).

DEMOS – Licence to Publish

THE WORK (AS DEFINED BELOW) IS PROVIDED UNDER THE TERMS OF THIS LICENCE ("LICENCE"). THE WORK IS PROTECTED BY COPYRIGHT AND/OR OTHER APPLICABLE LAW. ANY USE OF THE WORK OTHER THAN AS AUTHORIZED UNDER THIS LICENCE IS PROHIBITED. BY EXERCISING ANY RIGHTS TO THE WORK PROVIDED HERE, YOU ACCEPT AND AGREE TO BE BOUND BY THE TERMS OF THIS LICENCE. DEMOS GRANTS YOU THE RIGHTS CONTAINED HERE IN CONSIDERATION OF YOUR ACCEPTANCE OF SUCH TERMS AND CONDITIONS.

1. **Definitions**
   a **"Collective Work"** means a work, such as a periodical issue, anthology or encyclopedia, in which the Work in its entirety in unmodified form, along with a number of other contributions, constituting separate and independent works in themselves, are assembled into a collective whole. A work that constitutes a Collective Work will not be considered a Derivative Work (as defined below) for the purposes of this Licence.
   b **"Derivative Work"** means a work based upon the Work or upon the Work and other pre-existing works, such as a musical arrangement, dramatization, fictionalization, motion picture version, sound recording, art reproduction, abridgment, condensation, or any other form in which the Work may be recast, transformed, or adapted, except that a work that constitutes a Collective Work or a translation from English into another language will not be considered a Derivative Work for the purpose of this Licence.
   c **"Licensor"** means the individual or entity that offers the Work under the terms of this Licence.
   d **"Original Author"** means the individual or entity who created the Work.
   e **"Work"** means the copyrightable work of authorship offered under the terms of this Licence.
   f **"You"** means an individual or entity exercising rights under this Licence who has not previously violated the terms of this Licence with respect to the Work, or who has received express permission from DEMOS to exercise rights under this Licence despite a previous violation.
2. **Fair Use Rights.** Nothing in this licence is intended to reduce, limit, or restrict any rights arising from fair use, first sale or other limitations on the exclusive rights of the copyright owner under copyright law or other applicable laws.
3. **Licence Grant.** Subject to the terms and conditions of this Licence, Licensor hereby grants You a worldwide, royalty-free, non-exclusive, perpetual (for the duration of the applicable copyright) licence to exercise the rights in the Work as stated below:
   a to reproduce the Work, to incorporate the Work into one or more Collective Works, and to reproduce the Work as incorporated in the Collective Works;
   b to distribute copies or phonorecords of, display publicly, perform publicly, and perform publicly by means of a digital audio transmission the Work including as incorporated in Collective Works;
   The above rights may be exercised in all media and formats whether now known or hereafter devised. The above rights include the right to make such modifications as are technically necessary to exercise the rights in other media and formats. All rights not expressly granted by Licensor are hereby reserved.
4. **Restrictions.** The licence granted in Section 3 above is expressly made subject to and limited by the following restrictions:
   a You may distribute, publicly display, publicly perform, or publicly digitally perform the Work only under the terms of this Licence, and You must include a copy of, or the Uniform Resource Identifier for, this Licence with every copy or phonorecord of the Work You distribute, publicly display, publicly perform, or publicly digitally perform. You may not offer or impose any terms on the Work that alter or restrict the terms of this Licence or the recipients' exercise of the rights granted hereunder. You may not sublicence the Work. You must keep intact all notices that refer to this Licence and to the disclaimer of warranties. You may not distribute, publicly display, publicly perform, or publicly digitally perform the Work with any technological measures that control access or use of the Work in a manner inconsistent with the terms of this Licence Agreement. The above applies to the Work as incorporated in a Collective Work, but this does not require the Collective Work apart from the Work itself to be made subject to the terms of this Licence. If You create a Collective Work, upon notice from any Licencor You must, to the extent practicable, remove from the Collective Work any reference to such Licensor or the Original Author, as requested.
   b You may not exercise any of the rights granted to You in Section 3 above in any manner that is primarily intended for or directed toward commercial advantage or private monetary

compensation. The exchange of the Work for other copyrighted works by means of digital file-sharing or otherwise shall not be considered to be intended for or directed toward commercial advantage or private monetary compensation, provided there is no payment of any monetary compensation in connection with the exchange of copyrighted works.

c   If you distribute, publicly display, publicly perform, or publicly digitally perform the Work or any Collective Works, You must keep intact all copyright notices for the Work and give the Original Author credit reasonable to the medium or means You are utilizing by conveying the name (or pseudonym if applicable) of the Original Author if supplied; the title of the Work if supplied. Such credit may be implemented in any reasonable manner; provided, however, that in the case of a Collective Work, at a minimum such credit will appear where any other comparable authorship credit appears and in a manner at least as prominent as such other comparable authorship credit.

5.   Representations, Warranties and Disclaimer

a   By offering the Work for public release under this Licence, Licensor represents and warrants that, to the best of Licensor's knowledge after reasonable inquiry:

i   Licensor has secured all rights in the Work necessary to grant the licence rights hereunder and to permit the lawful exercise of the rights granted hereunder without You having any obligation to pay any royalties, compulsory licence fees, residuals or any other payments;

ii   The Work does not infringe the copyright, trademark, publicity rights, common law rights or any other right of any third party or constitute defamation, invasion of privacy or other tortious injury to any third party.

b   EXCEPT AS EXPRESSLY STATED IN THIS LICENCE OR OTHERWISE AGREED IN WRITING OR REQUIRED BY APPLICABLE LAW, THE WORK IS LICENCED ON AN "AS IS" BASIS, WITHOUT WARRANTIES OF ANY KIND, EITHER EXPRESS OR IMPLIED INCLUDING, WITHOUT LIMITATION, ANY WARRANTIES REGARDING THE CONTENTS OR ACCURACY OF THE WORK.

6.   Limitation on Liability. EXCEPT TO THE EXTENT REQUIRED BY APPLICABLE LAW, AND EXCEPT FOR DAMAGES ARISING FROM LIABILITY TO A THIRD PARTY RESULTING FROM BREACH OF THE WARRANTIES IN SECTION 5, IN NO EVENT WILL LICENSOR BE LIABLE TO YOU ON ANY LEGAL THEORY FOR ANY SPECIAL, INCIDENTAL, CONSEQUENTIAL, PUNITIVE OR EXEMPLARY DAMAGES ARISING OUT OF THIS LICENCE OR THE USE OF THE WORK, EVEN IF LICENSOR HAS BEEN ADVISED OF THE POSSIBILITY OF SUCH DAMAGES.

7.   Termination

a   This Licence and the rights granted hereunder will terminate automatically upon any breach by You of the terms of this Licence. Individuals or entities who have received Collective Works from You under this Licence, however, will not have their licences terminated provided such individuals or entities remain in full compliance with those licences. Sections 1, 2, 5, 6, 7, and 8 will survive any termination of this Licence.

b   Subject to the above terms and conditions, the licence granted here is perpetual (for the duration of the applicable copyright in the Work). Notwithstanding the above, Licensor reserves the right to release the Work under different licence terms or to stop distributing the Work at any time; provided, however that any such election will not serve to withdraw this Licence (or any other licence that has been, or is required to be, granted under the terms of this Licence), and this Licence will continue in full force and effect unless terminated as stated above.

8.   Miscellaneous

a   Each time You distribute or publicly digitally perform the Work or a Collective Work, DEMOS offers to the recipient a licence to the Work on the same terms and conditions as the licence granted to You under this Licence.

b   If any provision of this Licence is invalid or unenforceable under applicable law, it shall not affect the validity or enforceability of the remainder of the terms of this Licence, and without further action by the parties to this agreement, such provision shall be reformed to the minimum extent necessary to make such provision valid and enforceable.

c   No term or provision of this Licence shall be deemed waived and no breach consented to unless such waiver or consent shall be in writing and signed by the party to be charged with such waiver or consent.

d   This Licence constitutes the entire agreement between the parties with respect to the Work licensed here. There are no understandings, agreements or representations with respect to the Work not specified here. Licensor shall not be bound by any additional provisions that may appear in any communication from You. This Licence may not be modified without the mutual written agreement of DEMOS and You.